Wayland £8.99 HE006419, 780.92

D1807845

8012

FAMOUS
MUSICIANS

Joanne Jessop

Wayland

Famous people

Famous Artists
Famous Campaigners for Change
Famous Explorers
Famous Inventors
Famous Musicians
Famous Scientists

Picture acknowledgements
The publishers would like to thank the following for supplying pictures:
All-Action Pictures 32, 35/Lee Brookes, 41, 42/D.Raban; Archiv für Kunst und
Geschichte, Berlin 5, 7, 8, 10, 12, 13, 15; Clive Barda 40, 42; Camera Press *cover*, 19,
21, 28, 30/Karsh of Ottawa, 31/P.Francis, 33/Daniel Kramer, 34 & 37/John
Launois; Mary Evans 9, 14, 17; Ronald Grant Archive 22; Hulton Deutsch
Collection 23, 26, 38; Peter Newark 20, 24; Popperfoto 36, 39; Redferns 29/
S.Morley; Sefton Samuels *cover*, 41; Syndication International 27; Topham 25, 45;
Wayland Picture Library *cover*, 4, ll/D.Cumming; Zefa 6, 16, 18.
Cover artwork by Peter Dennis.

Series and book editor: Rosemary Ashley
Series designer: Malcolm Walker

First published in 1993 by
Wayland (Publishers) Limited
61 Western Road, Hove
East Sussex, BN3 lJD, England

© Copyright 1993 Wayland (Publishers) Limited

British Library Cataloguing in Publication Data
Jessop, Joanne
  Famous Musicians. -(Famous People Series)
  I. Title   II. Series
  780.92

ISBN 0-7502-0886-4

Typeset by Kudos Editorial and Design Services
Printed and bound in Italy by Rotolito Lombarda S.p.A, Milan

Contents

Introduction

Throughout history, music has had an important place in people's lives. It is a special language, capable of expressing our deepest emotions. The language of music is constantly changing, as musicians of all kinds produce new compositions, new techniques and new interpretations of familiar sounds.

This book looks at twelve musicians who have each made a unique contribution to the world of music. Their contributions have included beautiful works by composers such as Mozart, Beethoven and Chopin; inspired performances by musicians like Jacqueline du Pré and Luciano Pavarotti, and thrilling sounds from jazz innovators such as Louis Armstrong and Billie Holiday. Others have reflected the mood and tastes of society, and provided us with new, popular sounds. All the musicians in this book have become famous for their originality and skill.

Wolfgang Amadeus *Mozart*

Musical genius

Mozart began playing the harpsichord at the age of three and gave his first public performance when he was five. He went on to become one of the greatest of all geniuses. His music still ranks as some of the best ever composed. Yet throughout his musical career Mozart had to struggle to make a living as a performer and composer. When he died at the age of thirty-five, he was buried in an unmarked pauper's grave.

Wolfgang Amadeus Mozart is considered by many to be the world's greatest composer. He was undoubtedly a musical genius. In his short life, he produced over six hundred pieces of music, including operas, orchestral symphonies, and concertos for many different instruments, including piano, violin, flute and horn.

Mozart was born in 1756 in Salzburg, Austria, into a musical family. His father, Leopold, worked as a musician in the court of the Archbishop of Salzburg. As a young child, Wolfgang taught himself to play the harpsichord by listening to his older sister, Maria Anna, as she practised her lessons. By the age

Mozart as a young boy. His amazing musical talent became obvious from a very early age.

At the age of six, Wolfgang and his sister, Maria Ana, were taken on a musical tour of Europe by their father. They became known as the 'wonder children'.

of four, he was playing little pieces, and even composing tunes with help from his father. Leopold Mozart realized that his son was a child prodigy, and he tried to do everything he could to develop his son's talent. When Wolfgang was six and Maria Anna was ten, Leopold took them on tours to perform in the major cities of Europe. The 'wonder children', as they became known, were a great hit wherever they went.

Mozart's talent astounded everyone. By the time he was seven he was composing music in his head, and playing it before he knew how to write it down. At the age of eight he wrote his first symphony; at eleven his first opera. Leopold Mozart was amazed at his son's progress, saying 'God performs new miracles every day through this child'.

In 1779, when Mozart was twenty-three, he took a job as organist at the court of the Archbishop of Salzburg. Musicians in those days were treated as servants and were expected to adapt their music to the wishes of their employers. Mozart

hated to be restricted in this way, so in 1781 he resigned from the Archbishop's service and moved to Vienna to try to make his own way as a performer and composer. This was a brave move for a musician.

In Vienna, Mozart's reputation grew. His music was published and his operas were performed. He married Constanza Weber in 1782. During their marriage they had several children, of whom two survived.

Unfortunately, Mozart's musical achievements did not bring financial security. There were no copyright laws to protect his musical compositions, so he did not always receive payment for the publication or performance of his work. Sometimes audiences were unable to appreciate the brilliance of his music; the Austrian Emperor once commented after the first performance of a new opera that it had 'too many notes'. In spite of these setbacks, Mozart continued to pour out music. He often worked as if inspired, hearing a complete composition in his head before writing it down. He was known to arrive at a concert and play his own part from memory because he had not had time to write the music down. He worked extremely fast and seldom made changes

Mozart's operas are still favourites with audiences today. This is a modern production of The Magic Flute.

once a piece was finished. During a six-week period in the summer of 1788, Mozart wrote his last three symphonies – Nos 39, 40 and 41 (the 'Jupiter'). These are regarded as some of the finest music ever written.

One day in 1791, a stranger visited Mozart and asked him to compose a requiem. The man paid well but he would not reveal his identity because he wanted to pass the music off as his own. Mozart was ill at the time and was convinced that someone was trying to poison him. He became obsessed with the Requiem, thinking of it as his own death music. Mozart died on 5 December, aged thirty-five. The unfinished Requiem was completed by one of his students. There were many rumours after his death that Mozart had been poisoned. But there is no proof of this and it seems likely that he died from natural causes.

Dates

1756 born in Salzburg, Austria, on 27 January
1763-6 taken on concert tour with his sister Maria Anna
1767-79 concert tours
1779 takes a job as organist at the Court of the Archbishop of Salzburg
1786 first performance of the opera *The Marriage of Figaro*
1787 first performance of the opera *Don Giovanni*
1788 composes last three symphonies – nos 39, 40 and 41 (Jupiter)
1791 first performance of the opera *The Magic Flute*; begins composing the Requiem; dies on 5 December

This painting shows Mozart on his death bed, trying to finish The Requiem. *He died before it was completed.*

Ludwig van *Beethoven*

Music's heroic figure

Beethoven was one of the greatest of all classical composers. His music is filled with powerful emotions and feelings. He was also a talented pianist, and his often wild appearance and rough manners surprised and excited the people of Vienna, where he lived. Sadly, at the age of thirty, he began to lose his hearing. But in spite of increasing deafness, Beethoven continued to write beautiful and stirring music. His last symphony, the 'Choral' Symphony, was written when he was completely deaf.

Ludwig van Beethoven was born in 1770 in Bonn, Germany. Like Mozart, he came from a musical family. His father, Johann, was a musician in the court of the Elector, or Prince, in Bonn. However, Johann was not a particularly talented musician or even a good father, and he tended to bully rather than encourage his son to practise the violin.

Young Ludwig's creative talents did not flourish under his father's harsh discipline.

A portrait of Beethoven when he was forty-nine. By now he had become almost completely deaf.

But when he was eleven, he started lessons with Christian Gottlieb Neefe, the organist at the Elector's court. It was his teacher's gentle guidance and encouragement that awakened Beethoven's interest in music, and his talents began to blossom. By the age of twelve, Beethoven was writing pieces of piano music. At thirteen he had become Neefe's assistant organist.

In 1792, at the age of twenty-two, Beethoven moved to Vienna to make his living as a musician. He was an excellent pianist, playing with such feeling and emotion that he could move audiences to tears of sadness or lift their spirits in joy. He became a popular performer and was generally thought of as Vienna's finest pianist.

But it was not just Beethoven's music that drew people's attention; everything about him caused amazement in Viennese society. His untidy clothes and his shock of thick black hair stood out in sharp contrast to the elegant finery and powdered wigs that were the fashion of the day. Beethoven was a somewhat arrogant and head-strong character who was often rude and bad-tempered with people. He considered himself a musical genius who should be allowed to create music on his own terms, without being hurried or influenced by the wishes of a patron. Fortunately, Beethoven's talents as a pianist and composer were so impressive that in spite of his

awkward personality and independent attitude he found several wealthy patrons who were willing to support him while he wrote his music.

In 1800, when Beethoven was thirty years old and had published his first symphony, he realized that he was gradually losing his hearing. Deafness put an end to Beethoven's career as a pianist, but it caused him to concentrate all his energies on composing. As his deafness increasingly cut him off from the world around him, his music became more expressive of his inner feelings. Beethoven wrote some of his best-known works at this time, including the Fifth and Sixth

Symphonies. The Fifth Symphony is famous for its simple but compelling opening notes. The Sixth, or 'Pastoral', Symphony was an entirely new kind of symphony in which Beethoven used music to create images of the countryside; there are the sounds of a babbling brook, singing birds and a violent thunderstorm.

For Beethoven, music was a way of expressing his innermost feelings. In this respect, his music marks a break from the traditional Classical style of music, which was more concerned with form and structure. Although Beethoven was a master of the Classical style, his music had the expressive qualities characteristic of the Romantic movement, which was beginning to influence European music, literature and painting.

By 1820 Beethoven was totally deaf. Despite this handicap, he composed some of his greatest works. One

of the most famous was the Ninth Symphony, also known as the 'Choral' Symphony. This introduced singers into a symphony for the first time and needed an orchestra twice the size of any used before.

Beethoven continued to write beautiful music and had started work on his tenth symphony when he became seriously ill. In March 1827 he became unconscious. According to some accounts, he was lying on his deathbed when there was a loud clap of thunder. He sat upright, shook his fist at the sky and fell back dead!

Frédéric *Chopin*

Master of the piano

Chopin was one of the greatest composers of music for the piano. He was also a fine pianist, performing concerts and demonstrating to audiences the full range and power of the piano, which in his day was a new and modern instrument. Chopin was born in Poland and he spent most of his life in France. But he never forgot his native country and he often used rhythms and melodies from Polish folk music in his works.

Frédéric Chopin was a talented pianist and one of the greatest composers of music for the piano.

Frédéric Chopin was born near Warsaw, Poland, on 22 February 1810. His father was a Frenchman who had settled in Poland; his mother was Polish.

Chopin, like Mozart, first showed his musical genius when as a young child he began to imitate his older sister as she practised on the piano. He was composing musical pieces before he understood how to write them down. By the time he was eight he gave his first public concert. He was only fifteen when one of his compositions was published.

In 1829, when Chopin was nineteen, he went on a concert tour. He was so well received in Paris that he decided to live there, and he never returned to Poland. However, the folk music of his native land had a great influence on his musical style; rhythms and melodies of two Polish dances, the mazurka and polonaise, can be heard in many of his compositions.

In Paris, Chopin was in great demand as a performer and teacher. Because of his shy and retiring nature, he avoided big concert performances, preferring to play for smaller audiences in the homes of wealthy people.

The instrument that Chopin played, and composed most of his music for, was the piano. This was a new instrument that was just becoming popular. It had a greater range and depth of sound than the harpsichord, which it replaced. The advantage of the piano over the harpsichord was that its strings were struck with a felt-tipped hammer. This produced a fuller, less tinny sound than the harpsichord, in which the strings were plucked. The piano player could also control the loudness and softness of each note. Chopin developed a mastery of the piano, playing with a passionate yet delicate touch, delighting his audiences. All his compositions included the piano, and most were short pieces for piano alone.

Chopin worked slowly, constantly rewriting and perfecting his compositions. His beautiful piano pieces earned him the reputation as the greatest composer for the piano; to this day, his music is enjoyed by players and listeners everywhere.

J. BRANDARD, DEL ET LITH.   M & N. HANHART, CHROMOLITH.

THE BOHEMIAN POLKA,
BY
KŒNIG.

ENT. STA. HALL.   P. 3/.

Many of Chopin's compositions reflect the influence of the rhythms and melodies of the folk dances of his native Poland.

Chopin moved in the most fashionable circles of Paris society, mixing with many leading writers and artists. For over ten years he lived with Aurore Dudevant, who wrote novels under the pen-name George Sand. She was a famous figure in Paris, who believed that women should be able to live as freely as men, and she behaved according to her beliefs. For instance, she wore trousers and smoked in public, which in the mid-nineteenth century was considered outrageous behaviour for a woman. George Sand was a strong-willed and forceful person, who handled the practical side of life for the impractical and indecisive Chopin. This arrangement allowed Chopin to concentrate on his music. But eventually conflicts arose between these two very different personalities and they parted in 1848.

Chopin had never been strong, but his health declined rapidly after his separation from George Sand. He developed tuberculosis, a lung disease, and died on 17 October 1849. He was thirty-nine years old. According to his wishes, his heart was taken back to be buried in his beloved Poland.

Dates

1810 born near Warsaw, Poland, on 22 February
1817 writes his first composition
1818 gives his first public concert
1825 his first composition is published
1831 arrives in Paris
1836 meets George Sand
1848 relationship with George Sand ends
1849 dies on 17 October

This painting shows Chopin just before he died. Death is shown as a grim black figure, waiting at the window while Chopin plays his piano for the last time.

Peter Illich *Tchaikovsky*

Music of joy and sorrow

Tchaikovsky wrote some of the best-loved melodies of all time. His music was full of passion and feeling; it could excite audiences or move them to tears. His ballet music is some of the happiest and most tuneful music ever written.

Although he was a famous and admired musician, Tchaikovsky was a deeply sensitive man who suffered from periods of depression, an illness of the mind. He died, perhaps by suicide, at the age of fifty-three, at the height of his fame.

By the end of his life, in the late nineteenth century, Peter Illich Tchaikovsky was acknowledged as the greatest living composer. However, at the beginning of his career, his compositions were not always well received. Tchaikovsky's music, which is so popular and familiar today, was at the time considered to be very modern and different. Some people thought it was too sentimental and emotional. But audiences everywhere soon came to appreciate Tchaikovsky's distinctive musical style, which was full of passion and feeling.

By the end of his life, when this portrait was painted, Tchaikovsky was considered to be the greatest living composer.

Tchaikovsky was born in Votkinsk, Russia, in 1840. His parents had no particular ambitions for their son to become a musician, but young Peter showed an early interest in music. He was given piano lessons at the age of five and within a year he could play better than his teacher. His mother died when he was fourteen and he was greatly saddened by her death. He began to compose music which, he said, 'helped to sooth his troubled mind'.

At the age of nineteen, Tchaikovsky started work as a government clerk in St Petersburg, studying music in his spare time. After four years, he left his job to become a full-time student at St Petersburg Conservatory. He graduated with honours and was immediately offered a post at the Moscow Conservatory, where he taught for the next twelve years. During this period, Tchaikovsky's compositions were greeted sometimes with harsh criticism but more and more often with admiration.

Among Tchaikovsky's admirers was a wealthy widow named Madame Nadezhda von Meck. In 1877, she offered Tchaikovsky a yearly sum of money so that he could continue his work without financial worries, but only on the understanding that they would never meet. Their pen-friendship lasted fourteen years and during this period they exchanged about 3,000 letters. Many of these letters remain as important records of Tchaikovsky's thoughts and methods of composition.

Also in 1877, Tchaikovsky met and married Antonia Milukov. This was an impulsive marriage based on a very short acquaintance. The marriage proved to be a disaster; Antonia was a very unstable person, and Tchaikovsky

Above   A Russian ballerina dances the role of Odette in Swan Lake, *Tchaikovsky's much-loved and most famous ballet.*

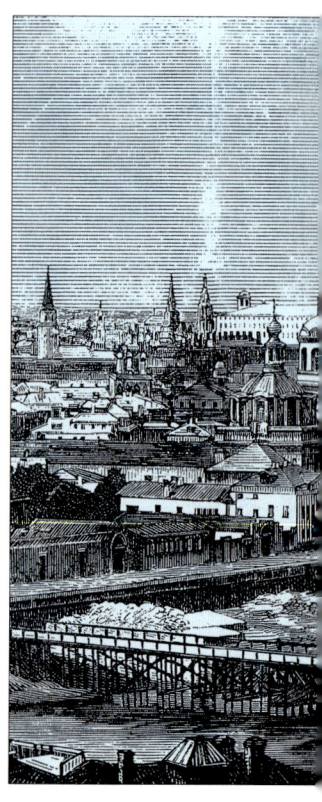

was unsuited for married life. Within three months the couple had separated. Tchaikovsky was deeply unhappy after this experience. He resigned from the Moscow Conservatory and settled in the peace of the countryside to devote himself entirely to composing.

Tchaikovsky was a composer in the Romantic tradition, writing music that was full of personal feelings. In a letter to Madame von Meck he wrote that his compositions 'have all been *felt* and *lived* by me and come straight from the heart'. Tchaikovsky's music was often inspired by Russian folk tunes and the Russian influence can be heard in the lively and expressive quality of many of his pieces.

Tchaikovsky's music includes some of the world's best-loved melodies. Pieces such as the *Romeo and Juliet Fantasy-Overture* and his *First Piano Concerto* are great favourites. His ballets – *Swan Lake*, *Sleeping Beauty* and *The Nutcracker* – are considered masterpieces and are still among the most popular ballets. Almost everyone has heard his rousing *1812 Overture*, with its cannonfire for realistic sound effects, and his beautiful *Serenade for Strings*.

Moscow in the late 1800s, where Tchaikovsky was Professor of Harmony at the Music Conservatory.

A scene from Tchaikovsky's ballet Sleeping Beauty, *which is still one of the most popular ballets of all time.*

Between 1888 and 1893 Tchaikovsky toured Europe and the USA, conducting his own works. In 1890, Nadezhda von Meck ended her correspondence without a word of explanation, leaving Tchaikovsky deeply hurt and upset.

In 1893, Tchaikovsky conducted the first performance of his Sixth Symphony. He called it the 'Pathétique' (full of feeling), saying, 'It is based on so much emotion and feeling that when I composed this work I found myself crying.' Tchaikovsky considered this to be his greatest composition; it was also his last. Less than two weeks later he was dead. At the time it was thought that he died of cholera, a disease caused by contaminated water, but recent evidence suggests that he may have committed suicide by drinking poison.

Dates

1848 born in Votkinsk, Russia on 7 May
1863 studies at the St Petersburg Conservatory
1866 becomes Professor of Harmony at the Moscow Conservatory
1877 receives pension from Madame von Meck; marries and separates from Antonia Milukov
1878 resigns from Moscow Conservatory and moves to the country
1888-93 tours Europe and USA
1893 composes the Sixth (Pathétique) Symphony

Louis 'Satchmo' Armstrong

King of jazz

Louis Armstrong was born in 1900 in New Orleans, Louisiana, the birthplace of jazz. His genius for improvisation, or playing music on the spur of the moment, and his unique style as a trumpeter had an important influence on the development of jazz and helped to make this form of music popular with the public. He died in 1971, and he is still considered one of the greatest jazz musicians.

Louis Armstrong, unlike the other musicians we have discussed so far, did not show any great musical ability at an early age. This was not because he lacked talent but because he lacked opportunity. Louis Armstrong was born in 1900 into a poor black family in New Orleans in the southern USA. With no money to spare for instruments or lessons, Louis's musical experience was limited to singing on

The famous 'Satchmo' smile.

the streets as a child, for which he earned a little money. But when Louis was thirteen, something happened that was to change his life and, as a consequence, was to have a profound influence on the world of music.

On New Year's Eve, 1913, Louis was arrested for firing a revolver in the street and sent to a 'Home for Coloured Waifs' (homeless black children). There he was given a cornet and a place in the band. Louis's natural talents began to flourish; within a few weeks he was leader of the band. The Waifs' Home gave Louis not only his start in music but also his nickname. The other boys called him 'Satchelmouth' because of his large mouth; this was later shortened to 'Satchmo', a name that stuck for the rest of his life.

The King Oliver's Creole Jazz Band in 1920. Louis Armstrong, shown kneeling at the front, played with this band during his teenage years in New Orleans. Later he joined Oliver in Chicago, where the band and Armstrong became the most exciting attraction of Chicago night life.

When Satchmo was released from the Home after serving his eighteen-month sentence, he played the cornet in various local bands, improving his techniques and becoming quite well known in his home town. He spent a couple of seasons in the early 1920s playing in a band on a paddle-steamer that travelled along the Mississippi River. The bands Armstrong played with were creating a new sound that was to become known as jazz.

In the Deep South, where black and white people were kept apart (segregated), black people had few opportunites for formal music training, so over the years they had developed their own kinds of music. Some of their music was slow and mournful like the blues; some of it was lively and spirited like ragtime. Jazz was a blend of these different kinds of music, set to a strong rhythm and syncopated (unaccented) beat. But most exciting of all, jazz was improvised music. As the musicians played, they would make changes to the tune or even make up entirely new tunes as they went along.

By the late 1920s, Satchmo was playing with the top jazz bands in Chicago, where he exchanged his cornet for a

Louis Armstrong became even more famous with appearances in more than fifty Hollywood films. He is shown here with Bing Crosby in a scene from the film High Society.

trumpet, and was being hailed as the world's greatest trumpeter. He was a great improvisor and could turn an ordinary tune into a moving instrumental piece. At first, jazz was ensemble music with all the musicians playing together, but audiences were soon clamouring for Satchmo's solo performances. He invented 'scat singing' – using nonsense syllables to imitate the sounds made by various instruments. Jazz musicians everywhere were adopting the Armstrong style, but Satchmo remained the greatest of them all.

By the 1930s, jazz had entered the mainstream of 'respectable' music, and Satchmo was jazz's biggest star, touring the USA and Europe. His fame increased with his appearances as musician and actor in over fifty Hollywood films. He was still performing when he died from a heart attack in 1971. Music lovers everywhere mourned the loss of the 'king of jazz'.

Dates

1900 born in New Orleans, Louisana, USA, on 4 July
1913 arrested and sent to 'Home for Coloured Waifs' where he learns to play the cornet
1914 released from the home and starts playing in local bands
1921 joins a band on paddle-steamer travelling along the Mississippi River
1922 moves to Chicago
1932 first European tour
1936 appears in his first Hollywood film, *Pennies from Heaven* with Bing Crosby
1971 dies

Billie *Holiday*

Unique jazz singer

Billie Holiday was a talented jazz singer. She sang with great expression and feeling and had a sense of timing and phrasing that turned simple songs into musical poetry. In spite of her talents, Billie Holiday suffered many personal sorrows in her life, from which she tried to escape with drugs and alcohol. These eventually ruined her singing career and brought about her death at the age of forty-four.

Billie Holiday is considered by many to be the greatest jazz singer. Her remarkable gift was not the power or range of her voice but rather her unique style of singing. With a slight alteration in the phrasing of the lyrics and subtle changes in the harmony, she could transform a simple sentimental song into a moody sound full of deep feelings.

Billie Holiday was born in 1915 in Baltimore, Maryland, in the USA, where she grew up in extreme poverty. When she was twelve she moved to New York City to be with her

Billie Holiday started her career as a night-club singer in Harlem, New York's black district. As her popularity grew, she was offered singing engagements in the city's 'white' clubs.

At the height of her career, Billie Holiday performed in concert halls and on radio and television.

mother. She was soon drawn to Harlem, the black district of the city, where the clubs and night-spots were humming with the sounds of jazz. Billie had no musical education but she had a great love for jazz. While still in her teens, she started singing in the night-clubs of Harlem. Her songs expressed deep-felt emotions that spoke directly to her audiences, and her reputation as a singer of rare quality soon spread among jazz enthusiasts. In 1933 she made her first record, with Benny Goodman. There were more recording sessions to come, and more performances at night-clubs and concert halls and on radio and television.

Throughout her career, Billie was faced with the humiliations and frustrations of racial prejudice and discrimination. She performed at many 'whites only' clubs, where her black friends could not come to hear her and she was not allowed to mingle with the customers after her performances. In 1937, she travelled with the Count Basie Orchestra to the southern states of the USA, where blacks and whites were not allowed to perform together. Here she had to 'black-up' (darken her skin with make-up) in case she was mistaken for white. The following year, when she travelled with Artie Shaw's band, she often found herself

Dates

1915 born in Baltimore, Maryland, USA, (date uncertain)
1927 moves to New York City
1930 begins singing at night-clubs in Harlem
1933 makes her first record, with Benny Goodman
1947 serves prison sentence for possession of illegal drugs
1954 first European tour
1959 second European tour; 17 July dies in hospital

seperated from the rest of the band because she was barred from 'whites only' restaurants and hotels. When she appeared with Louis Armstrong in *New Orleans*, her only film apprearance, she played a maid and he was a butler – the only roles Hollywood considered suitable for black people.

Suffering from the hurts of racial discrimination and from several unhappy relationships with men, Billie turned more and more to alchohol and drugs to escape her sadness and disappointments. In 1947 she was sent to prison for possessing illegal drugs. She never completely kicked her drug habits, and in the last ten years of her life her voice and her health suffered. Although her voice was weakened, she never lost the marvellous sense of timing and the soulful interpretation of songs that had made her one of the finest jazz singers. Billie Holiday continued to perform to appreciative audiences in the USA and made two successful European tours.

Eventually drugs and alcohol took their toll; in June 1959, Billie Holiday became unconscious and was taken into hospital. There she had to face the shame of being arrested for possession of drugs. Too ill to be moved, she was placed under police guard. She died on 17 July 1959 at the age of forty-four.

Above left Billie Holiday during her last European tour.

25

Elvis *Presley*

King of rock'n'roll

Elvis Presley was born in America's Deep South into a poor white family. He rose from poverty to become the 'king of rock'n'roll' and one of the most famous people in the world. But fame eventually destroyed him. He became addicted to pills to help him sleep and pills to help him lose weight, and he died at the age of forty-four.

Elvis Presley was the first rock'n'roll superstar. He entered the music scene in 1954 and by 1956 he was possibly the most famous man in the world. Elvis Presley had a sound and style that thrilled the young and scandalized their elders. He swivelled his hips, fell to his knees and snarled into the microphone. His long hair and sideburns and his fantastic outfits started a fashion craze. Everywhere he went he was mobbed by screaming fans; his live performances sent audiences wild with excitement and caused teenage girls to faint.

'Elvis the Pelvis' during a performance. He was nicknamed this because of the way he swivelled his hips while playing the guitar and singing into the microphone.

Elvis's outrageous stage performances delighted his young fans but upset many of their elders.

Young people everywhere were swept up by 'Elvis-mania'.

There was nothing in his background to indicate that Elvis Presley would become a famous musician. He was born in 1935 in Tupelo, Mississippi, in the southern USA. His childhood was one of extreme poverty. As a boy he sang in the church choir. When he was ten he entered a talent contest and won second prize for his singing. On his eleventh birthday Elvis was given a guitar. There was no money for lessons, so he taught himself to play. He particularly liked to imitate the rhythm and blues sound of black musicians.

In 1948, Elvis and his parents moved to Memphis, Tennessee, where his father hoped to find work. Elvis finished school at eighteen and took a job as a truck driver. At that time he had no thoughts of becoming a professional musician, but he still played and sang for his own pleasure. In 1953, he went to the Memphis Recording Service to make a private record of his singing to give to his mother as a birthday gift. Then fate stepped in.

Elvis signing autographs. Wherever he went he was mobbed by crowds of adoring fans.

At that time, racial prejudice was so strong that many white people would not buy records by black musicians, even if they liked the music. The president of Memphis Recording Service was looking for a white man who sang like a black man. When by chance he heard the recording of Elvis, he knew he had found his man. He arranged for Elvis to make a record with a back-up group. This was the first time that Elvis had played with other musicians. The record they made was played on local radio stations and became an instant hit in Memphis. With the success of the record came live performances. During 1954 and 1955, Elvis and his band played all over the states of Texas and Mississippi.

In 1955, Elvis was taken in hand by a manager named Colonel Tom Parker, who promoted the singer to the rest of the nation and the world. In 1956 Elvis Presley became an international star with his hit songs *Heartbreak Hotel* and *Blue Suede Shoes*. These were followed by more hit recordings, live performances, television appearances and then films.

In 1958, at the height of his career, Elvis was called up for service in the US army. His famous sideburns were cut off, his hair trimmed, and 'Private Presley' was posted to Germany. He left the army in 1960 with a new, clean-cut image and a more subdued singing style. Gone were the sideburns, the flamboyant outfits and the outrageous stage performances.

For the next five years Elvis concentrated on films, starring in a series of second-rate Hollywood movies. In 1967 he married Priscilla Beaulieu, whom he had met when he was stationed in Germany. The marriage lasted for five years. In 1968 he made a comeback on TV, complete with long hair and black leather and singing the old favourites.

During the 1970s there were many elaborate stage shows, with magnificent costumes that were designed to hide his increasing bulk. His voice was still strong but the sparkle had gone out of Elvis's performances. He was overweight and addicted to prescription drugs such as diet pills and sleeping pills. On 1 August 1977, he was discovered unconscious at his home in Memphis. He was rushed to hospital but his life could not be saved. At forty-four, the 'king of rock'n'roll' was dead.

Dates

1935 born at Tupelo, Mississippi, on 8 January
1948 moves with his parents to Memphis, Tennessee
1953 makes a record for his mother's birthday
1954 makes his first commercial record
1955 Colonel Tom Parker becomes Elvis's manager and promoter
1956 records his first hit record – *Heartbreak Hotel*; starts his movie career
1958 is called up for service in the US army
1967 marries Priscilla Beaulieu
1968 makes a TV comeback
1977 dies in Memphis on 16 August

During the 1970s, Elvis made a comeback, appearing in many elaborately staged live shows.

Luciano *Pavarotti*

International opera star

Luciano Pavarotti is one of the world's most famous opera singers. He has done much to take opera out of the opera houses and into the everyday lives of thousands of fans. When he sang *Nessun Dorma* at the opening of the football World Cup in 1990, he made it one of the best-loved opera songs of all time.

Pavarotti is considered to have one of opera's finest tenor voices.

Luciano Pavarotti is one of the world's greatest tenors, and certainly the most famous. His ability to reach the highest notes of a tenor range and the purity of his tone have earned him the title of 'King of the high Cs'. His wonderful singing and the warmth and charm of his personality have made him an international star whose popularity extends far beyond the opera world.

Pavarotti was born in 1935 in Modena, Italy. His father was a baker who enjoyed singing, and he passed on his love of singing to his son. Young Luciano enjoyed listening to his father's records of great tenors and was soon trying to imitate them. When he was barely five years old he would take his toy mandolin into the courtyard of the block of flats where his family lived and serenade the neighbours. They rewarded him with applause and a shower of sweets thrown from the balconies.

In 1954, Pavarotti finished school and had to decide whether to train to become a teacher or a singer. A career as a teacher offered security, but, with the support of his family, Pavarotti decided to try his luck as a professional singer. So in 1954, at the age of nineteen, he started to study singing with teachers in Modena and later in Mantua. During his training period, he worked part-time in the local school as a teaching assistant and later sold insurance to help support himself.

By 1961, Pavarotti had sung in a few concerts but had not made it professionally as a singer. He was very discouraged and almost ready to quit. But that year his luck changed. He entered a singing competiton and won first prize. The prize was the opportunity to appear in a production of Puccini's

One of Pavarotti's many performances as Rodolfo in Puccini's La Bohème.

opera *La Bohème*. Pavarotti was a great success in the opera, and his career prospects looked much brighter. Five months after his opera debut, Pavarotti was married. He and his wife Adua remain happily married and have three daughters.

Over the next few years, Pavarotti sang in opera houses throughout Europe. But, as is often the case with opera singers, it took a long time before he became known, even in the opera world. In 1965, he toured Australia with the Australian soprano Joan Sutherland and her opera company. In 1968 he made his American debut.

Since then Pavarotti's popularity as a fine tenor has continued to grow. He is admired everywhere for his great operatic roles, and also for his concert and television performances, where he is able to reach audiences who might otherwise never hear or see opera. His stirring singing of *Nessun Dorma* from the opera *Turandot* by Puccini at the televised opening of the 1990 World Cup games in Rome won him a place in the hearts of millions of viewers throughout the world. Every Pavarotti concert closes with this great love song, which has become his trademark.

Dates

1935 born in Modena, Italy, on 12 October
1954 starts voice training
1961 wins singing competition and lead role in *La Bohème*; marries Adua Veroni
1965 Australian tour
1968 American tour
1990 sings *Nessun Dorma* at the 1990 World Cup concert in Rome

Bob *Dylan*

Folk poet

During the early 1960s, Bob Dylan's protest songs, full of poetry and emotion, captured the spirit of the time. By the mid-1960s, Dylan had given up his role as a protester and switched to rock'n'roll and later to country and western music. His conversion to Christianity in the late 1970s was reflected in the gospel style of many of his songs. He has since returned to his Jewish faith. He remains a popular song-writer and poet.

Right   Bob Dylan was the most famous folk singer of the 1960s. His poetic lyrics expressed the mood of the young and captured the spirit of his generation.

During the early 1960s, Bob Dylan used his music to protest against social injustice, racial prejudice and war. Like all true folk music, Dylan's songs expressed the feelings and views of a particular group of people – those young people who were angry and frustrated with the way their society was run. His poetic lyrics captured the mood of the rebellious 1960s so well that Bob Dylan became known as the 'spokesman for a generation'.

Bob Dylan began his life as Robert Zimmerman. He was born in the USA in 1941 and grew up in Hibbing, Minnesota. He had little training in music but during his teens he played in many rock'n'roll bands. He wanted to get away from the closeness and small town atmosphere of Hibbing. In 1959 he went to university in Minneapolis, Wisconsin. While at university he adopted a new musical style – folk music. He learned to play the guitar and the harmonica, and started to perform at local coffee houses. He also chose a new name, after the Welsh poet Dylan Thomas, whom he greatly admired.

In 1961, Dylan left university and headed for New York City to make his way in the music world. He became a popular figure in New York coffee houses and became known as the rising star of folk music. Dylan was a unique performer. He delivered his songs in a flat, almost conversational style of singing, and between songs he would entertain his audiences with long, rambling stories.

By 1962, his talents as a poet were being expressed in an outpouring of protest songs. In 1963, when he sang *Blowin' in the Wind* and *The Times They Are A-Changin'* at the Newport Folk Festival in the USA, he was a huge success. He became the most popular figure in the world of folk music and the symbol of social and political protest.

But Dylan did not like to be restricted to a particular style of music or by his role as social protester. At the 1965 Newport Folk Festival, he sang a blend of folk and rock'n'roll music backed up by an amplified rock band. Although some of his

Right Dylan's musical style has undergone many changes over the years. His guitar and harmonica have been replaced by more up-to-date electric instruments.

Left Bob Dylan and Joan Baez in 1964. The names of these two folk singers were often linked together, both musically and personally.

earlier fans were upset, the switch to 'rock' increased his popularity as a singer.

In 1966 Dylan had a serious motorcycle accident and spent several years recovering, away from the public eye. When he returned to the music scene he had taken on yet another style – country and western. During the 1970s he experimented with many different styles of music. The Dylan of the 1970s was more concerned with personal feelings than political causes. He also tried new forms of communication, appearing in the film *Pat Garrett and Billy the Kid*, for which he wrote and sang most of the music. He also wrote two books, *Tarantuala* and *The Writing and Drawing by Bob Dylan*. In the late 1970s Dylan, who had been born into the Jewish faith, became a Christian. His albums and concerts during this period celebrated his new-found religion. By 1983, he had returned to the Jewish faith. Bob Dylan remains a popular performer and song-writer, and probably the finest rock poet.

The *Beatles*

The 'Fab Four'

The Beatles were probably the most famous pop group. They began their career in 1960 in Liverpool, England, and by 1964, 'Beatlemania' had swept the nation and spread to the rest of the world. During their ten years together, the Beatles' music matured from simple rock songs to sophisticated melodies and lyrics. They wrote nearly two hundred songs in a wide variety of styles, many of which remain favourites today.

In 1961, a little-known pop group called The Beatles was playing in a club in Liverpool. One night, Brian Epstein, the owner of a local record shop, went to see them and realized that here was something special. He offered to become their manager and set the group on the road to fame. But no one could ever have imagined just how famous the Beatles would become. Within a few years, the four Beatles – John Lennon, Paul McCartney, George Harrison and Ringo Starr – were international celebrities, creating a sensation wherever they went. The frenzy and adoration they inspired among their fans became known as Beatlemania.

The Beatles of the early 1960s presented a clean-cut, fun-loving image. From left to right they are; Paul McCartney, George Harrison, Ringo Starr and John Lennon.

They first made it to the charts with *Love Me Do*, a song written by Lennon and McCartney. This was soon followed by more hit tunes by the Lennon-McCartney song-writing team. The Beatles' music had a fresh, lively quality that the fans loved. Their concerts were packed with frantic fans; girls screamed and wept when they appeared on stage. By 1964 Beatlemania had spread to the USA and the rest of the world. The group broke all records for concert attendance and record sales. They produced one hit song after another; they made three successful films. Everywhere they went they were mobbed by adoring fans; everything they did was a success.

By 1966, the Beatles had had enough of frenzied crowds and stopped giving concerts; they wanted to concentrate on making albums. The frantic days of Beatlemania had ended and the group entered a more mature phase of their career. They set up their own record company, Apple, so that they could have complete freedom to create their own music.

None of the Beatles, except George, had any formal musical training, but with the help of their record producer George Martin, who was trained in classical music, they were able to expand the range of their music. They adapted classical techniques and introduced electronic music. They were constantly trying out new techniques and approaches to

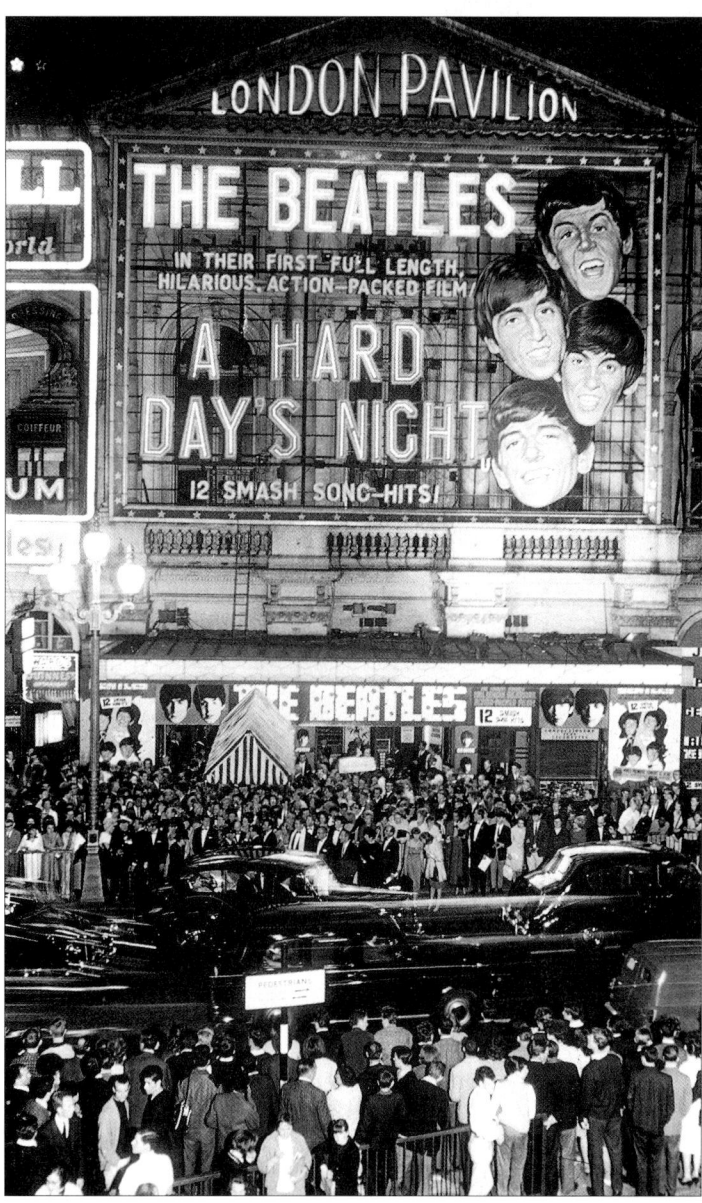

Thousands of fans wait outside the cinema before the first showing of the Beatles' film A Hard Day's Night.

Above By the late 1960s the Beatles' image had changed, as had their music. The group had acquired a 'hippie' look and their music had progressed from simple pop songs to more complex melodies, and lyrics that drew attention to the social issues of the day.

songs. The music of the Beatles progressed from simple pop songs to more sophisticated and complex melodies. Their lyrics, too, became more poetic and they often sang about social issues.

By 1970 the four Beatles were going their own separate ways and the group was disbanded, never to perform together again. John Lennon continued to write songs and recorded with his wife, Yoko Ono. In 1980 he was shot dead outside his New York home. Paul McCartney continues a hugely successful career, writing music and performing in concerts all over the world. George Harrison also writes and performs music and has become a successful film producer.

Dates

1960 the Beatles are formed in Liverpool, England
1961 Brian Epstein becomes their manager
1962 their first hit single, *Love Me Do*
1964 Beatles' records become hits in the USA; US tour; film *A Hard Day's Night*
1965 film *Help!*; awarded MBEs by Queen Elizabeth II
1966 stop all concert tours and concentrate on making albums
1967 film *The Magical Mystery Tour*
1970 the group splits up
1980 John Lennon murdered in New York

Jacqueline *du Pré*

Virtuoso cellist

Jacqueline du Pré was one of the world's greatest cellists. She played with great skill and sensitivity. Her marriage to the pianist Daniel Barenboim was seen as a fairy-tale romance between two gifted musicians. Jaqueline's playing career was tragically cut short when she developed multiple sclerosis, a disease that made it impossible for her to handle her cello. She taught other musicians until her death in 1987, at the age of forty-two.

Jacqueline du Pré was a cellist of outstanding talent. Her playing was filled with energy and passion and her body and her instrument seemed to work together as one, to produce exquisite music.

Jaqueline du Pré was born in 1945 in Oxford, England, and grew up in Putney, south London. When she was four she started playing pieces on the piano after hearing her older sister at her lessons. Just before her fifth

Jacqueline du Pré began playing the cello when she was five. By the age of sixteen, she had started on a career as an international concert cellist.

In 1967, du Pré married the pianist Daniel Barenboim. Their wedding took place at the end of the Arab-Israeli Six Day War in Israel, during which they toured the country giving concerts in support of the war effort. The marriage of these two talented musicians in such dramatic circumstances had a fairy-tale charm.

birthday, she heard a cello on the radio and was immediately attracted to the sound. She told her mother, 'I want to make that sound.' Jacqueline was given cello lessons and every encouragement to develop her interest. Her mother, herself a talented musician, would compose little cello pieces at night and leave them by her daughter's bedside. Jacqueline loved to wake up to these surprises and would run to her cello to practise them.

When she was eleven, Jacqueline won a scholarship to study the cello. One condition of the scholarship was that she practise for four hours each day. Schooling and playtime had to fit around her cello lessons and practise time. This demanding schedule left little time to play with other children and set her apart from her classmates. Jacqueline was a shy girl and was often lonely, but she found comfort in her greatest friend, her cello. 'I would tell it all my sadness and my problems. It gave me everything I needed and wanted.'

At sixteen, she made her concert debut at Wigmore Hall in London. Her playing was greatly admired, and before long Jacqueline was living the hectic life of an international concert player.

In 1967 she met the Israeli pianist and conductor Daniel Barenboim. There was an immediate attraction between these two very gifted musicians, and soon they were engaged to be married. Their wedding plans were disrupted by the outbreak of war between Israel and the Arab nations. Barenboim felt his place was with his country in its time of need. He and Jacqueline flew to Israel and gave performances all over the country in support of the war effort. On 15 June 1967, shortly after the fighting had stopped, Jaqueline and Daniel were married.

Daniel Barenboim and Jacqueline du Pré were called 'the golden couple' and their marriage was seen as the 'musical love match of two child prodigies'. They were a very happy, loving couple and travelled and performed together whenever they could.

Within a few years of her marriage, Jacqueline started to suffer from occasional tingling sensations and numbness in her fingers. Often she felt extremely tired. Her doctor diagnosed the problem as nervous strain and sent her to a psychiatrist. She continued to perform and tried to keep up with her energetic husband. But sometimes performances had to be cancelled because Jacqueline could not control her hands or legs.

In 1973 Jacqueline was rehearsing for a performance in New York when her

Jacqueline du Pré played with great feeling. Her body and her cello seemed to move together as one instrument, to produce exquisite music.

symptoms returned. Her fingers felt numb and she could not control her bow properly. She wanted to cancel the performance but was told it was merely an attack of nerves and was persuaded to play. She gave a disappointing performance and then cancelled all other engagements. This was to be her last public performance.

The doctors still diagnosed the problem as stress. It was only after several more months of tests that it was found that she was suffering from an illness called multiple sclerosis – the problem was her body and not her mind.

There was a gradual decline in Jacqueline's health. Eventually she lost complete control in her arms and legs. When she could no longer play her beloved cello, she gave lessons. Near the end of her life new symptoms appeared; she suffered from blurred vision and tremors of the head, making it impossible even to read or watch television. Jacqueline du Pré died in 1987, aged forty-two.

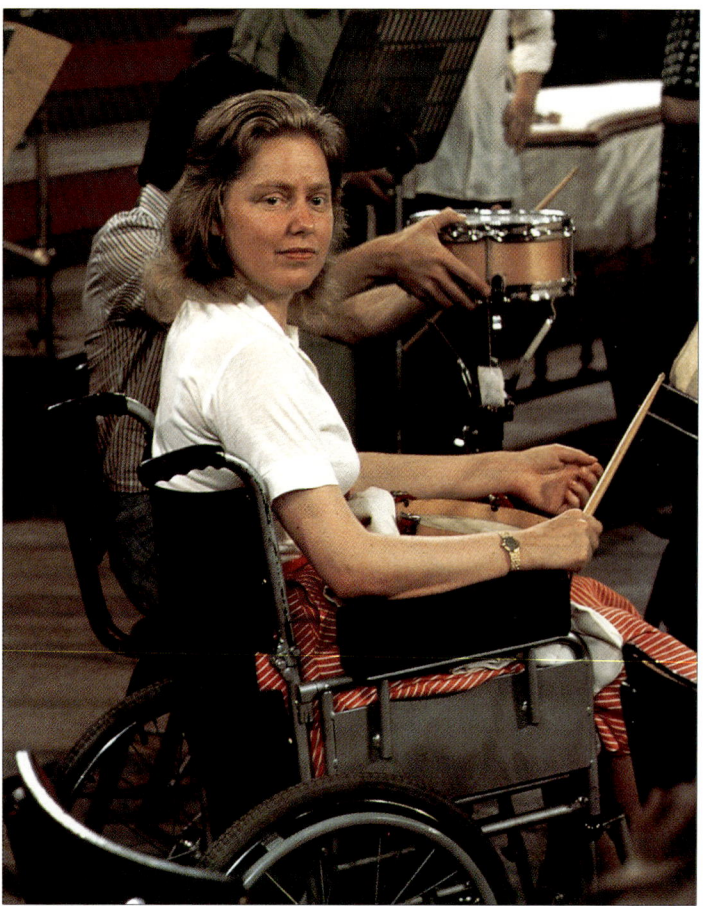

Dates

1945 born in Oxford, England on 26 January
1948 moves with her family to South London
1950 starts cello lessons
1956 wins a scholarship to study the cello
1961 concert debut
1967 meets and marries Daniel Barenboim
1973 her last public performance; told she has multiple sclerosis
1987 dies on 19 October

When her illness meant that she could no longer handle her cello, Jacqueline du Pré gave lessons to other musicians.

Madonna

Pop superstar

Madonna is the world's most famous entertainer. She began her career as a pop singer and through talent, sheer determination and hard work, soon reached the rank of superstar. Although some of her songs and videos have not always been well received – they are sometimes felt to be a bad influence on her young fans – such criticism has served to make her even more famous.

Madonna Louise Ciccone, known simply as Madonna, is the best-known entertainer in the world today.

Madonna was born in 1959 in Rochester, Michigan, in the USA, into a large Italian-American family. She has five older brothers and two younger sisters. Madonna's mother died when she was six and two years later her father re-married.

Madonna, the singer, song-writer, actress and clever business woman.

Madonna was interested in dance from an early age, and when she finished high school she won a place at the University of Michigan to study dance. She stayed at the university for only one year and then headed for New York City, hoping to become a star. During her early years in New York, Madonna lived in the poorest neighbourhoods and took odd jobs to support herself as she studied dance. Soon, she switched from dancing to singing. She learned to play the drums and sang in several rock bands in New York and also began to write her own songs. Madonna had great ambition and drive, and by 1983 she had been taken on by a record company who produced her first album, *Madonna*.

After the success of her album, she hired Michael Jackson's manager, Freddy DeMann, to promote her. With his help, Madonna was on her way to becoming a superstar. She had a series of hit singles, albums and music videos. Her first music video, *Like a Virgin*, filmed in 1984, caused a stir because of its sexy lyrics and images. But Madonna seems to thrive on being outrageous. Her live performances and videos often use a blend of sexual and religious images that many people find offensive. Many parents see Madonna as a bad influence on their children. However, criticism does not lessen her popularity with her fans; it simply makes sure that Madonna is the centre of a great deal of attention.

Madonna's costumes are often as outrageous as her lyrics.

Madonna in performance during her 'Blond Ambition' tour.

In 1984 Madonna turned her attention to films – the pop star wanted to become a movie star. Her first starring role was in the film *Desperately Seeking Susan*. In 1985 she married actor Sean Penn, and they starred together in *Shanghai Express*. She has since appeared in several other films. In 1991 she made a documentary called *In Bed with Madonna*, which shows the behind-the-scenes life of one of her concert tours. Once again Madonna caused a sensation by the explicit and, as some thought, tasteless nature of the film.

Madonna has proved to be a hard-headed business woman. She is the head of Madonna Inc., a large corporation that employs hundreds of people to promote Madonna and her music. She is now the biggest-earning female performer in the USA.

Dates

1959 born in Rochester, Michigan, USA on 16 August
1977 wins a scholarship to study dance
1978 leaves university and moves to New York City; studies dance
1979-82 sings with various groups
1983 first album, *Madonna*
1983 first starring role in the film *Desperately Seeking Susan*; makes sexually explicit music video *Like a Virgin*
1986 stars in *Shanghai Express* with Sean Penn
1990 stars in *Dick Tracy* with Warren Beatty
1991 makes controversial film *In Bed with Madonna*
1992 stars in the film *A League of Their Own*
1993 her controversial book *Sex* is published

Glossary

Amplified   Electronically increased sound.

Blues   A style of music that began with black musicians in the USA. Blues is characterized by its slow tempo and sad lyrics, and its particular harmony.

Classical music   Music composed during the second half of the eighteenth century, known as the 'Classical Period'. During this time people looked back to the days of Ancient Rome and Greece for their inspiration in music, painting and literature.

Concerto   A musical composition for a solo instrument and orchestra. A concerto usually has three separate movements, or parts.

Conservatory   A music school.

Copyright laws   Laws protecting the exclusive right to reproduce music, works of art and literature, etc.

Cornet   A brass instrument similar to a trumpet.

Country and western   A type of rural folk music that began in the American West and was originally sung to guitar music.

Debut   A musician's first public appearance.

Ensemble   The French word for 'together'; as a musical term it refers to music that is played together by several musicians or to the group of musicians playing together .

Harmony   The sound of two or more notes together.

Folk music   The traditional music of a particular group or community, often passed down from one generation to another. Today the folk music of North America is especially popular; it retains the traditional forms that developed in the 1880s and early 1900s and is played with a strong rhythmic beat on acoustic (non-electric) instruments such as guitar or harmonica.

Improvised   Music composed as the musician plays.

Jazz   A type of improvised music with a syncopated beat and a strong rhythm developed in the southern USA by black musicians in the early 1900s. Jazz was based on blues, ragtime and brass band music of the Deep South.

Lyrics   The words of a song.

Mandolin   A musical instrument played by plucking the strings.

Multiple sclerosis   A disease of the central nervous system that causes the gradual loss of the use of muscles.

Opera   A stage play that is sung to orchestral music. The first opera dates from around 1600.

Overture   A piece of music played at the beginning of an opera or play; also an independent piece of music suggested by a play or novel.

Patron   Someone who sponsors and helps a musician or other artist.

Pauper   A person who is extemely poor.

Phrasing   The division of a short piece, or phrase, of music.

Prodigy   A person, usually a child, who is extraordinarily talented.

Racial discrimination Unfair treatment of a person or people.

Racial prejudice Intolerance or dislike of people of a specific race, religion, etc. – usually of white people for black people.

Ragtime A type of music characterized by a syncopated beat in fast regular time. Ragtime was developed among black musicians in the southern USA and was popular from about 1890 to 1915.

Requiem The music to be played at a mass for the dead.

Rock'n'roll A form of popular music with a strong, regular beat. It developed from jazz and blues.

Romantic music Most music written between 1800 and 1900, when composers cared less about rules and more about the mood or feeling in their music.

Segregated To be kept apart from others.

Solo A musical piece for a single instrument or voice or a performance by one person.

Sonata A musical composition for piano or for a solo instrument with piano accompaniment written in three or four movements.

Symphony A musical composition for orchestra in four separate movements.

Syncopated beat Beats that are placed on the normally unaccented notes.

Technique The way in which a skilled performance is carried out.

Tenor A male singer whose voice has a range between high (alto) and low (baritone).

Virtuoso A person who has supreme musical skill and artistry.

Books to read

Beethoven by Alan Blackwood (Wayland, 1987)
Dylan: Behind the Shades: by Clinton Heylin (Penguin, 1991)
Elvis Presley by Vanora Leigh (Wayland, 1986)
Frederyk Chopin by Richard Tames (Franklin Watts, 1991)
Jacqueline du Pré by Carol Easton (Hodder and Stoughton, 1989)
Music by Alan Blackwood (Wayland, 1988)
Music and Musicians by Eva Bailey (Batsford, 1983)
Music, an Illustrated Encyclopedia by Neil Ardley (Hamlyn, 1986)
Mozart by Percy Young (Wayland, 1987)
Pavarotti: My Own Story by Luciano Pavarotti and William Wright (Sidgwick and Jackson, 1981)
Tchaikovsky by Elizabeth Clark, (Wayland, 1988)
Twenty Names in Classical Music by Alan Blackwood (Wayland, 1987)
Twenty Names in Pop Music by Andrew Langley (Wayland, 1987)

Index